This Love is Forever

A book for children of divorce and their parents

Written by Mavis Prall Cohen

Illustrated by Lizzie Prall

Published by Semaphore Media

ISBN 978-0-615-64664-0

Some kids have moms and dads who live together.
Some kids' parents stay married forever.

But sometimes grown-ups feel that
a marriage is through.
So instead of just one house, my family has two.

Divorce means that moms and dads live apart.
And for lots of kids, that split can be hard.

I get a kiss goodnight from one or the other.
This weekend from father, next weekend from mother.

The divorce had nothing to do with me.

If they could stay together, that's how it would be.

They tried to fix the problems they had.
They tried not to feel unhappy or mad.

But there are some problems that
just can't be fixed.

Some marriages break,
and there's no fix-it trick.

They made me from the love they once shared.
That love has changed—but I know they still care.

It's just that now they are more like friends.
And they can't live together once the marriage ends.

My family is different now, that's plain to see.

But what matters most is the way they love me.

They want me to be happy,
on that they're agreed.

They spend lots of time thinking
about what I need:

How to give me enough of their time.
How to make sure I know we'll all be fine.

My mom says she's still glad
she married my dad.
"Just look at the wonderful
child we had!"

"I know this is tough, and it's okay
to feel sad. Just know that we'll
love you forever," says Dad.

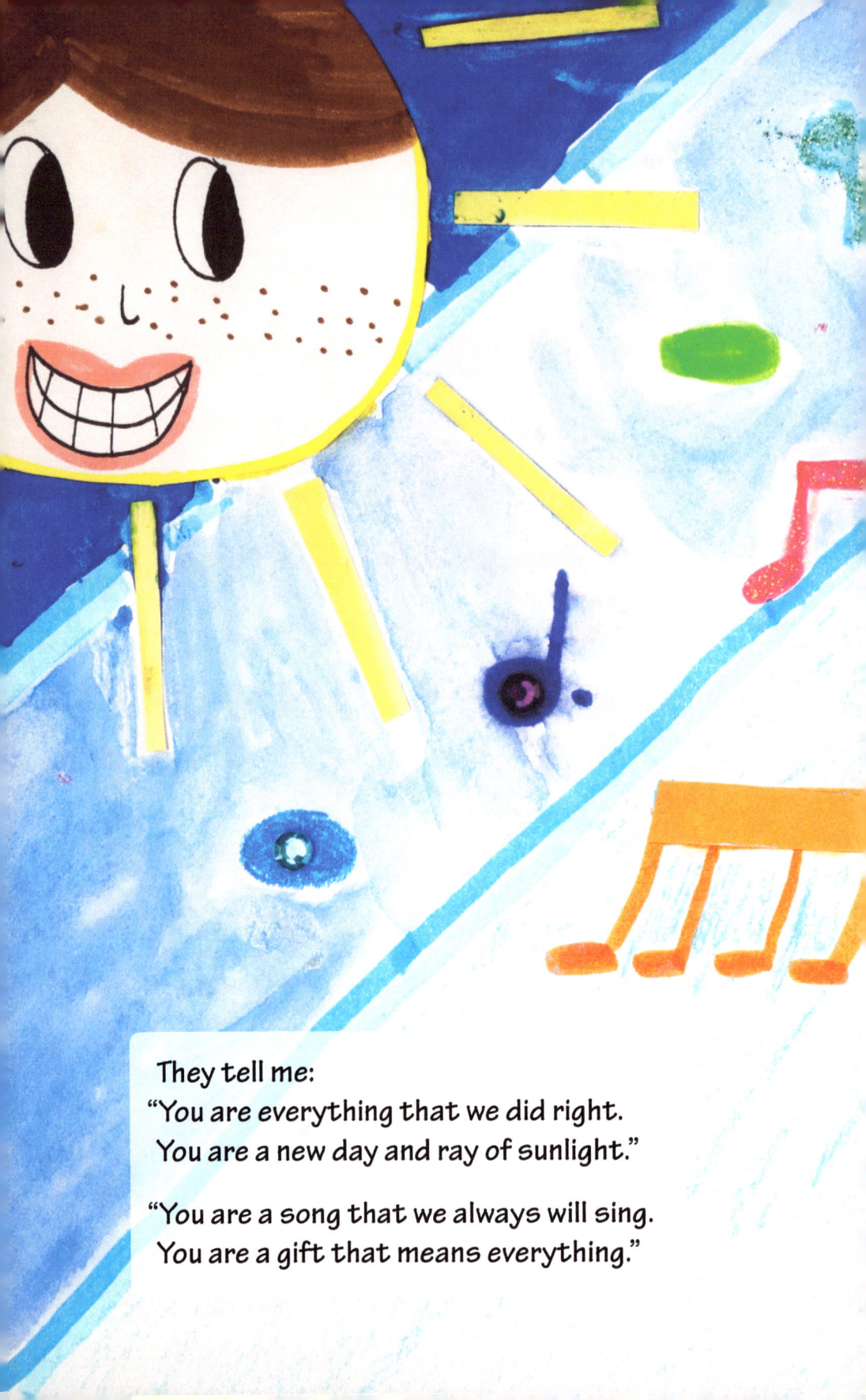

They tell me:
"You are everything that we did right.
You are a new day and ray of sunlight."

"You are a song that we always will sing.
You are a gift that means everything."

I am the best part of the marriage you see,
The part that lives on is here, inside me.

I'm made from the best of my dad and my mom.
And I know that their love for me always goes on.

Moms and dads don't always stay together.

But parents and children love each other forever.

ABOUT THE AUTHOR

Mavis Prall Cohen wrote *This Love is Forever* when her daughter Lizzie was three years old and asked, "Why are we divorced?" Mavis wanted to give Lizzie an answer she could understand, and that would also reassure her she would always be loved. As a child of divorce herself, Mavis felt she knew what Lizzie needed to hear, and Mavis wanted to create lasting messages that Lizzie could revisit as often as she liked. Mavis also found that the positive messages helped her, as a mom, stay focused on what matters most during times of turmoil: her child's well-being.

Mavis has a master's degree in journalism from Northwestern University. She began her career in TV news and then moved on to healthcare communications, later earning another master's degree from Northwestern University in Healthcare Quality and Patient Safety. She currently works in healthcare quality improvement for a large medical association. She and Lizzie live in the Chicago area with Mavis' husband and two step-daughters.

ABOUT THE ILLUSTRATOR

Lizzie Prall was one year old in 2000 when her parents split up, and at age three began asking her mother why the split had happened. Lizzie took comfort in the words her mother wrote for her, and years later when Mavis asked her to illustrate the book so that other families could benefit from its message, Lizzie happily agreed. Each of the illustrations is Lizzie's own creation, her vision of the words on the page. Lizzie has always enjoyed making art and is hoping this book will help other kids like her whose parents go through divorce.

We invite you to use the following pages to draw pictures of your own family. If you want to, you can share those pictures at ThisLoveIsForever.net.

www.ingramcontent.com/pod-product-compliance
Lightning Source LLC
Chambersburg PA
CBHW040348060426
42445CB00029B/41